LSD, PCP,
& Other
Hallucinogens

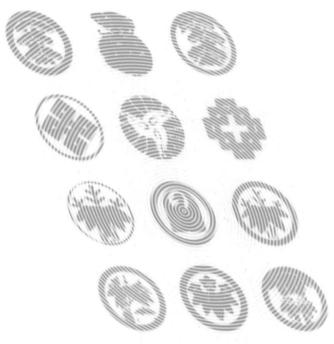

Junior Drug Awareness

Junior Drug Awareness

LSD, PCP, & Other Hallucinogens

Introduction by **BARRY R. McCAFFREY**
Director, Office of National Drug Control Policy

Foreword by **STEVEN L. JAFFE, M.D.**
Senior Consulting Editor,
Professor of Child and Adolescent Psychiatry, Emory University

Jane Ellen Phillips, Ph.D.

Chelsea House Publishers
Philadelphia

CHELSEA HOUSE PUBLISHERS
Editor in Chief Stephen Reginald
Production Manager Pamela Loos
Director of Photography Judy L. Hasday
Art Director Sara Davis
Managing Editor James D. Gallagher
Senior Production Editor LeeAnne Gelletly

Staff for LSD, PCP, AND OTHER HALLUCINOGENS
Senior Editor Therese De Angelis
Associate Art Director Takeshi Takahashi
Cover Illustrator/Designer Keith Trego
Editorial Assistant Jessica Carey
Produced by 21st Century Publishing and Communications, Inc.

Cover Photo © Tom Stewart/The Stock Market

The Chelsea House World Wide Website address is
http://www.chelseahouse.com

3 5 7 9 8 6 4 2

Library of Congress Cataloging-in-Publication Data
Phillips, Jane Ellen.
LSD, PCP, and other hallucinogenic drugs/Jane Ellen
Phillips.
80 pp.   cm. — (Junior drug awareness)
Includes bibliographical references and index.
Summary: Explains the different kinds of hallucinogenic
drugs, their history and effects, and how to get help in
remaining or becoming drug-free.
ISBN 0-7910-5183-8 (hc)
1. Hallucinogenic drugs—Juvenile literature. 2. Drug
abuse—Juvenile literature. [1. Hallucinogenic drugs. 2.
Drugs. 3. Drug abuse.] I. Title. II. Series.
HV5822.H25P48 1999
362.29'4—dc21   99-22299

CONTENTS

cooks books   16 96

4-16-d

by Barry R. McCaffrey
Director, Office of National
Drug Control Policy

STAYING AWAY FROM ILLEGAL DRUGS, TOBACCO PRODUCTS, AND ALCOHOL

G ood health allows you to be as strong, happy, smart, and skillful as you can possibly be. The worst thing about illegal drugs is that they damage people from the inside. Our bodies and minds are wonderful, complicated systems that run like finely tuned machines when we take care of ourselves.

Doctors prescribe legal drugs, called medicines, to heal us when we become sick, but dangerous chemicals that are not recommended by doctors, nurses, or pharmacists are called illegal drugs. These drugs cannot be bought in stores because they harm different organs of the body, causing illness or even death. Illegal drugs, such as marijuana, cocaine or "crack," heroin, methamphetamine ("meth"), and other dangerous substances are against the law because they affect our ability to think, work, play, sleep, or eat.

If anyone ever offers you illegal drugs or any kind of pills, liquids, substances to smoke, or shots to inject into your body, tell them you're not interested. You should report drug pushers—people who distribute these poisons—to parents, teachers, police, coaches, clergy, or other adults whom you trust.

Cigarettes and alcohol are also illegal for youngsters. Tobacco products and drinks like wine, beer, and liquor are particularly harmful for children and teenagers because their bodies, especially their nervous systems, are still developing. For this reason, young people are more likely to be hurt by illicit drugs—including cigarettes and alcohol. These two products kill more people—from cancer, and automobile accidents caused by intoxicated drivers—than all other drugs combined. We say about drug use: "Users are losers." Be a winner and stay away from illegal drugs, tobacco products, and alcoholic beverages.

Here are four reasons why you shouldn't use illegal drugs:

- Illegal drugs can cause brain damage.
- Illegal drugs are "psychoactive." This means that they change your personality or the way you feel. They also impair your judgment. While under the influence of drugs, you are more likely to endanger your life or someone else's. You will also be less able to protect yourself from danger.
- Many illegal drugs are addictive, which means that once a person starts taking them, stopping is extremely difficult. An addict's body craves the drug and becomes dependent upon it. The illegal drug–user may become sick if the drug is discontinued and so may become a slave to drugs.

- Some drugs, called "gateway" substances, can lead a person to take more-dangerous drugs. For example, a 12-year-old who smokes marijuana is 79 times more likely to have an addiction problem later in life than a child who never tries marijuana.

Here are some reasons why you shouldn't drink alcoholic beverages, including beer and wine coolers:

- Alcohol is the second leading cause of death in our country. More than 100,000 people die every year because of drinking.
- Adolescents are twice as likely as adults to be involved in fatal alcohol-related car crashes.
- Half of all assaults against girls or women involve alcohol.
- Drinking is illegal if you are under the age of 21. You could be arrested for this crime.

Here are three reasons why you shouldn't smoke cigarettes:

- Nicotine is highly addictive. Once you start smoking, it is very hard to stop, and smoking cigarettes causes lung cancer and other diseases. Tobacco- and nicotine-related diseases kill more than 400,000 people every year.
- Each day, 3,000 kids begin smoking. One-third of these youngsters will probably have their lives shortened because of tobacco use.
- Children who smoke cigarettes are almost six times more likely to use other illegal drugs than kids who don't smoke.

If your parents haven't told you how they feel about the dangers of illegal drugs, ask them. One of every 10 kids aged 12 to 17 is using illegal drugs. They do not understand the risks they are taking with their health and their lives. However, the vast majority of young people in America are smart enough to figure out that drugs, cigarettes, and alcohol could rob them of their future. Be your body's best friend: guard your mental and physical health by staying away from drugs.

WHY SHOULD I LEARN ABOUT DRUGS?

Steven L. Jaffe, M.D., Senior Consulting Editor,
Professor of Child and Adolescent Psychiatry,
Emory University

Your grandparents and great-grandparents did not think much about "drug awareness." That's because drugs, to most of them, simply meant "medicine."

Of the three types of drugs, medicine is the good type. Medicines such as penicillin and aspirin promote healing and help sick people get better.

Another type of drug is obviously bad for you because it is poison. Then there are the kinds of drugs that fool you, such as marijuana and LSD. They make you feel good, but they harm your body and brain.

Our great crisis today is that this third category of drugs has become widely abused. Drugs of abuse are everywhere, not just in rough neighborhoods. Many teens are introduced to drugs by older brothers, sisters, friends, or even friends' parents. Some people may use only a little bit of a drug, but others who inherited a tendency to become addicted may move on to using drugs all the time. If a family member is or was an alcoholic or an addict, a young person is at greater risk of becoming one.

Drug abuse can weaken us physically. Worse, it can cause

permanent mental damage. Our brain is the most important part of our body. Our thoughts, hopes, wishes, feelings, and memories are located there, within 100 billion nerve cells. Alcohol and drugs that are abused will harm—and even destroy—these cells. During the teen years, your brain continues to develop and grow, but drugs and alcohol can impair this growth.

I treat all types of teenagers at my hospital programs and in my office. Many suffer from depression or anxiety. A lot of them abuse drugs and alcohol, and this makes their depression or fears worse. I have celebrated birthdays and high school graduations with many of my patients. But I have also been to sad funerals for others who have died from problems with drug abuse.

Doctors understand more about drugs today than ever before. We've learned that some substances (even some foods) that we once thought were harmless can actually cause health problems. And for some people, medicines that help relieve one symptom might cause problems in other ways. This is because each person's body chemistry and immune system are different.

For all of these reasons, drug awareness is important for everyone. We need to learn which drugs to avoid or question— not only the destructive, illegal drugs we hear so much about in the news, but also ordinary medicines we buy at the supermarket or pharmacy. We need to understand that even "good" drugs can hurt us if they are not used correctly. We also need accurate scientific knowledge, not just rumors we hear from other teens.

Drug awareness enables you to make good decisions. It allows you to become powerful and strong and have a meaningful life!

Hallucinogens change users' views of the world around them, causing them to lose contact with reality. Users have described unreal, distorted, and frightening visions of themselves and others after taking hallucinogens.

WHAT ARE HALLUCINOGENS?

I was at a college party, and Ted, the guy who was in charge of making everyone's drinks, was an acquaintance of mine. I didn't like him very much. He was always making fun of what a nerd I was, telling me that I needed to "loosen up."

That night I decided to have a beer, so I asked Ted to pour one for me. He said he would have to go into the kitchen to get a glass for me and disappeared. When he came back he had my beer, and I was so thirsty that I took a couple gulps right away.

A few minutes later, I began to feel very strange. Instead of the usual "buzz" I got when I tried beer, I felt unsteady and unsure of where I was. The person hosting the party had a white sofa and a beautiful white rug. I was afraid I would vomit and ruin her furniture, so I decided to leave. But I couldn't find my coat, and after what seemed like a very long time, I just walked out without saying goodbye— and without finding my coat.

Once I got outside, I felt even more strange. I was very confused, but I also felt like the strongest person in the world. Nothing could harm me, I thought. It was winter and the weather was terrible—an icy wind whipped around me. But I didn't care. I didn't even feel the cold.

I shared an apartment with a friend of mine in the large city where we lived. To get home, I had to go through a pretty rough neighborhood. It was very late, but instead of catching a cab or bus I started walking, even though I didn't feel sure of where I was going. Along the way, a huge man stopped me and asked if I could light his cigarette. I told him that he was an idiot and to go away. The man became angry and followed me for a long time, yelling at me. I walked by a trash can, and the wine and beer bottles inside looked so pretty that I had to stop and touch them.

Then I came to a bridge, and when I began to walk across it I thought about jumping off. I knew I could fly if I had to, so I wouldn't get hurt. The only thing that stopped me was that I didn't want to get wet when I landed. Maybe I could do it without getting wet, I thought. I pondered this for a long time before crossing the bridge and walking into a parking lot. There were cars coming down a blind ramp, and the drivers just missed me and angrily honked at me to get out of the way. I waved back, because I knew if they hit me I wouldn't get hurt. I would probably just dent their cars, I figured. And anyway, who cared?

After about four hours of wandering, I finally made it home. When I got there, I decided to make french fries. I *put a pan of oil on the stove, turned on the burner, and then forgot about it and went to bed. Fortunately, a neighbor smelled the smoke, ran up to my apartment (I left the door unlocked), and put the fire out. I never even woke up.*

The next day I felt very sick, so I skipped classes and stayed in bed. I couldn't figure out what was wrong with me—or why my kitchen was such a mess. After all, I had only had one beer at the party, and I never even finished it. Over time, as I started to remember more about that night, I became scared, and so I tried to forget about it.

*A few months later I ran into Ted, who had served me the beer. "Hey," he said. "How was your **trip**?" I didn't know what to say. I hadn't gone on a trip. Then he said, "That was some beer, huh? My friends and I put a little **PCP** in there to loosen you up. It sure seemed like it worked. I wish you would have hung around for a while, though. You would have been fun to be with."*

I just stood there, stunned. I had narrowly missed being hit by cars, thought about jumping off a bridge, and had nearly burned down my apartment building. I could have killed innocent neighbors. After that party, I felt strange, sick, and depressed for days. And Ted thought this was funny? I told him I never wanted to see or speak to him again, but he never seemed to understand what the problem was with "spiking" my drink.

Now whenever I go out, I don't drink anything that I don't get myself. That experience was so frightening that I will never forget it. I never want to be that out of control ever again.

—Naomi, 22

What Is PCP?

PCP (phencyclidine) and its "sister" drug, **LSD** (lysergic acid diethylamide), are among a group of drugs known as **hallucinogens.** Hallucinogens are substances that change the user's thoughts, mood, and perceptions. At high doses, they cause the user to experience **hallucinations**—objects or visions that are not real, but are perceived by a person who has a mental disorder or who is using drugs. As you can see from Naomi's story, hallucinogens can be extremely dangerous. Even worse, they can change your life and your mind even if you use them just once.

LSD and PCP are probably among the most well-known kinds of hallucinogens. They are **synthetic,** or man-made, drugs. Other substances in this category include **STP** (a nickname that stands for "serenity, tranquillity, and peace") and **MDA** (methylenedioxyamphetamine). Naturally occurring hallucinogens include drugs like **peyote** or **mescaline** (both found in the cactus plant) and **psilocybin** (found in certain types of mushrooms). Mescaline and psilocybin are not as **potent** as the synthetic hallucinogens, and the "high" that users get from them

Did You Know?

The word "hallucinogen" comes from the Latin word *alucinare,* which means "to wander in mind." Hallucinogens do just that—they cause users to see or experience things that are not real, or they distort their perception of reality. The experience is almost like having a dream from which you cannot awake.

Whether a hallucinogen user has a euphoric "trip" or a frightening one depends on several factors. How large is the dose? How powerful is the drug? Hallucinogenic experiences can also vary depending on the user's personality and the setting in which the drug is taken.

does not usually last as long.

The visions caused by these drugs can continue as long as the drug is in the user's body. Although some people have described the trip, or high resulting from using hallucinogens, as pleasant, others have had terrifying experiences. These episodes may also be frightening because they are out of the person's control. Some people who have experienced a **"bad trip"** have tried taking other substances to help stop the hallucinations, but until the body breaks down the drug, its effects will continue.

Hallucinogens have been called **psychedelic** (mind-expanding) drugs. Another term is **psychotomimetic drugs,** meaning that they cause a condition similar to mental illness. They have also been called illusinogens. These terms seem to imply that the drugs cause **psychosis**. But although chronic users of hallucinogens may develop symptoms similar to some mental disorders, an actual LSD high usually does not include auditory hallucinations the way a psychotic episode does. A person suffering from a psychotic disorder hears things that are not real. A person on an LSD trip has more of a series of visual hallucinations. You may have heard the term "psychedelic" used to refer to bright patterns or colors. This use of the term began because people who are high on LSD usually see very strong colors or see existing colors as brighter and more vivid than they actually are.

A yearly survey by the National Institute on Drug Abuse shows that beginning in 1992, the number of eighth, tenth, and twelfth graders using hallucinogens began to rise. In 1995, for example, 5 percent of eighth graders, 9 percent of tenth graders, and 13 percent of twelfth graders reported that they had tried hallucinogens.

How Do PCP and LSD Differ?

Both PCP and LSD produce hallucinations, but not exactly in the same way. Users of LSD mainly have visions that are rich in color and seem to stimulate other senses. They also hear sounds that don't exist, and they smell and taste things that aren't there. People high on LSD see distorted faces and hear others' voices as funny-sounding. LSD users lose track of time; they are unaware of how long they have been on a trip. Users have described a wide variety of experiences while under the influence of the drug. Some claim that their trips are interesting and beautiful, and believe that these trips help them be more creative or "expand their minds." Other trips are highly unpleasant—colors are painfully bright and sounds are loud and harsh. Ugly scenes appear, and they cannot be stopped. These bad trips are sometimes called **bummers.**

People who are high on PCP also experience hallucinations, but they are usually extremely unpleasant or even frightening. PCP users often feel extreme **paranoia** (a feeling that people are out to get you) and experience tremors (trembling or shaking) and blackouts. PCP is more than just a hallucinogen; it also lessens pain and acts as a stimulant. It is an extremely complicated drug that affects the brain in many ways.

People who use PCP have described a feeling of being outside of their bodies. A user who is high may look at his arms, for example, and not realize that they belong to him. He may be able to move his

Hallucinogens can alter the drug user's perceptions of time and space. A person high on a hallucinogen will view details and objects differently. He or she may hear music, carry on conversations with imagined people, and experience odors and tastes that are not rooted in reality.

hands, but he can't control what they do. Users also experience a sense of being superhuman—many people who are high on PCP believe that they can fly, walk into the path of a moving bus, or pick up a car without being hurt. The **anesthetic** (causing loss of feeling or consciousness) qualities of PCP make users insensitive to pain and thus more likely to be injured. During a PCP high, users can also become violent, disoriented, confused, and extremely dangerous to themselves and others.

Fortunately, these powerful and often terrifying effects have turned many people away from using PCP, and its popularity has decreased in recent years. Most people who try the drug don't become regular, or chronic, users, either because they are frightened by their initial experiences or because they don't survive them.

But a new generation of kids—you and your friends—have not heard much about the dangers of hallucinogens. You may not know about the harmful and sometimes permanent effects they can have on your mind and body. For this reason, more kids your age are beginning to try these dangerous substances.

This book will help you learn more about the hazards of using hallucinogens, and why it is never safe to take drugs of any kind without medical supervision. The more you know about harmful drugs like LSD and PCP, the better equipped you will be to make an informed decision to stay healthy and drug-free.

An ordinary nightmare is bad enough, but the nightmares and bizarre visions often caused by hallucinogens can be truly terrifying. Despite what some people believe, "natural" drugs that come from plants may have the same effect.

NIGHTMARES AND VISIONS

LSD and PCP are the most commonly used hallucinogens, but they are part of a broad category of drugs that cause a variety of physical and mental effects in users. Most hallucinogens, such as STP and MDA, are synthetic and are similar to LSD and PCP. But a few, such as mescaline and psilocybin, are derived from plants. It is important to be aware of what these substances are and what they can do to you.

Hallucinogens can be divided into three categories: LSD and similar drugs; **belladonna alkaloids,** or drugs derived from plants like jimsonweed; and **dissociative anesthetics,** including PCP.

LSD and Related Hallucinogens

The drugs in this category not only cause hallucinations but also act like **amphetamines**—drugs that stimulate the body by increasing heart rate and blood pressure and dilating (expanding) the breathing tubes in the lungs. Amphetamines cause a sense of energy and alertness in users. In high doses they produce a sense of euphoria, or intense well-being. But they can also be extremely dangerous: an overdose can overstimulate the heart and cause death.

Drugs that are similar to LSD and are manufactured in laboratories include the following:

- DMA (dimethyoxyamphetamine)
- DOM (dimethoxy-methylphenylipsopropylamine), or STP
- MDA (methylenedioxyamphetamine)
- MDMA (methylenedioxymethamphetamine), or Ecstasy

LSD is also known as "acid," "windowpanes," "blotter," and "cubes." Sometimes the drugs listed above are combined and taken together; for example, taking LSD with MDMA is known as "candy flipping." These substances, which are often referred to as designer drugs, may have very complicated names, but most of them are synthetic variations of natural substances like mescaline, the compound found in the peyote cactus. They are stronger and more **toxic** (poisonous) than mescaline, however.

You may have already heard of one of the drugs in this group: MDMA, or Ecstasy. Beginning in the 1980s, Ecstasy became popular among teens and young adults at all-night "raves," where users took it to stay awake and dance for hours. Before the dangers of Ecstasy were well-known, nightclubs in New York distributed it free to the first customers arriving at their clubs each night. Like most hallucinogens, however, the drug is now illegal.

Another synthetic drug with properties similar to LSD is **DMT** (dimethyltryptamine), which is sometimes called the "businessman's special" because it is considered a convenient and quick way to get high. DMT acts very quickly on the brain and is easily absorbed and broken down in the body. The high it produces is very brief, lasting about an hour.

The chemical structure of DMT is similar to that of a hallucinogen found in a South American plant. Natives once used this hallucinogen as snuff. They named the snuff *yopa*. This drug is now consumed as a tea or is sometimes mixed with marijuana and smoked. The hallucinations it produces are very likely to cause anxiety and fear.

Mescaline, another LSD-like drug, comes from the peyote cactus native to northwest Mexico. Native American tribes of the United States and Mexico have used mescaline for religious and medical purposes for generations. Mescaline's hallucinogenic effects are much milder than those of LSD. The drug is usually taken by chewing the dried "buttons" of the cactus or swallowing them whole. The drug is then absorbed in the stomach and intestines. Users often become nauseated after ingesting mescaline buttons. Hallucinations usually occur only after many buttons are swallowed. Sometimes mescaline is also made into a dry powder, or the buttons are sometimes infused in hot water and made into a tea.

Because the chemical structure of mescaline is similar to that of many amphetamines, it has many of the same effects on the body, including a rise in blood pressure and heart rate. At the same time, mescaline produces hallucinations similar to those produced by LSD.

Other naturally occurring hallucinogens are found in mushrooms. In fact, mushrooms that contain these substances are probably second in popularity only to LSD. They are also called "magic mushrooms" or "'shrooms." Like mescaline, these mushrooms are

Frank Drayish, shown here, is president of the Native American Church of North America. Members of the church, who are mostly Navajo people of the Southwest, use peyote as a ceremonial food in religious rites. Peyote was once banned, but its use in Native American religious rituals is now legal.

consumed during religious ceremonies for their hallucinogenic effects. This religious practice has a long history among natives of Mexico and other parts of Central America.

Mushrooms from the *Psilocybe* family contain many compounds, but only two are thought to be responsible for causing hallucinations: psilocybin and **psilocin**. It is probably psilocin that causes hallucinations when the mushrooms are ingested. In low doses, the mushrooms create feelings of relaxation, physical lightness or heaviness, and distorted perceptions, but they can also cause light-headedness, numbness in the tongue or mouth, tremors, sweating, nausea, and anxiety.

One of the greatest dangers of using mushrooms as hallucinogens is that this type of plant can easily be misidentified. In some cases, people have consumed mushrooms that they thought would cause hallucinations but they were poisoned instead. Another danger is that hallucinogenic mushrooms can produce terrifying trips. Some users report that they still have terrible memories of the fear they experienced during bad trips resulting from eating mushrooms.

Belladonna Alkaloids: Deadly Plants

Belladonna alkaloids may sound beautiful, but they are extremely dangerous—and often deadly— compounds found in plants. One common plant containing belladonna alkaloids is jimsonweed, a member of the nightshade family that has large white or violet trumpet-shaped flowers and foul-smelling foliage.

(Jimsonweed got its name from a famous poisoning incident that left settlers of the 17th-century Jamestown, Virginia, colony extremely ill. The settlers mistakenly ate the leaves of the plant in a salad.)

The plants or seeds that contain belladonna alkaloids produce a bizarre, dreamlike state when consumed, but the user does not remember the experience because the substances also cause amnesia (loss of memory). Two of the belladonna alkaloids that act this way are **atropine** and **scopolamine.** Atropine is sometimes used today in minute doses to treat asthma patients, but at high doses it is lethal. It raises heart rate, breathing, and body temperature to dangerous levels. Scopolamine, on the other hand, is thought to affect thought and perception.

Belladonna alkaloids can shut down important functions in the body and cause the heart and lungs to malfunction. The brain loses the ability to control the body's thermostat, and users can die from extremely high body temperatures. Belladonna alkaloids also prevent an important brain chemical, **acetylcholine,** from working properly. Acetylcholine regulates many of the **autonomic** (involuntary) activities of the body that keep us alive, such as breathing. Unfortunately, some kids have been hospitalized or have died from using belladonna alkaloids because they were not aware of the risks they were taking.

PCP and Ketamine

PCP, also known as "angel dust," is one of the most dangerous drugs known. (Other street names for PCP include "crystal," "wack," "rocket fuel," "ozone," "horse tranquilizer," "peace pill," and "loveboat.") It was originally marketed as an anesthetic, or pain reducer, but its hallucinogenic effects were so severe that physicians discontinued its use. **Ketamine,** which was also designed to be used as an anesthetic during surgery, is very similar to and acts almost like PCP. Also called "Special K," ketamine is now used as an anesthetic by veterinarians. Both drugs are extremely dangerous to humans.

Taking PCP or ketamine has the same effects as drinking alcohol, taking an amphetamine, and taking a hallucinogen all at the same time. Like other amphetamines and some hallucinogens, PCP not only raises blood pressure and body temperature to unsafe levels, but it also causes a kind of drunken state in users. Slurred speech, poor coordination, and drowsiness are common effects.

When high on PCP, a user becomes insensitive to pain. (Remember Naomi's story in chapter 1, where she was walking through the city in freezing temperatures without a coat?) PCP users also experience what is known as a **dissociative state,** in which they are completely out of touch with the world around them. People in this state may be aware of physical sensations, but their brains do not clearly translate these feelings. When patients were anesthetized with PCP during a hospital study, for example, they were awake and aware of the room around them, but they did not feel that they were a part of it.

Someone who is high on PCP may become aggressive

or agitated. At very high doses, PCP can cause the muscles of the body to become rigid; the user may slip into a coma or develop seizures. It's no wonder that PCP users are considered a danger both to themselves and to others around them.

Other Hallucinogens

Did you know that hallucinogens can also come from animals? A relatively unknown hallucinogen is the compound called **bufotenine,** which is secreted by certain types of toads, such as the cane toad and Colorado River toad. Strange as it may sound, people have been known to ingest bufotenine by licking these animals. Others squeeze the toads to release the liquid drug from a gland found on the animals' backs. Some users have even killed toads and then boiled them to isolate the hallucinogen.

This practice may sound amusing, but the effects of bufotenine are no laughing matter. Like many other hallucinogens, the drug raises the user's blood pressure and heart rate and causes blurred vision and cramped muscles. It may also cause temporary paralysis. The short-lived high that users get from bufotenine is hardly worth the risks to their health.

How Are Hallucinogens Used?

LSD is colorless, odorless, and tasteless. It is a very potent drug—a very small amount can produce a high. LSD can be used in capsule form, but it is mostly produced as a liquid, which is then added to squares of gelatin, soaked into small pieces of brightly colored blotter paper, or even added to the backs of postage stamps. A drug dealer can easily sell the papers or stamps to a user, who only has to lick the paper to get high.

Today, a single dose of LSD is about 10 to 80 micrograms (a microgram is one-millionth of a gram, an extremely small amount). During the 1960s, when LSD was much more popular, stamps would contain 100 to 200 micrograms of the drug. This may not seem like a big difference, but LSD is so potent that only 20

Sugar-cane farmers introduced the cane toad into South Florida in the early 1900s to control pests. People soon discovered, however, that the toad secreted a fluid, bufotenine, that was hallucinogenic for humans. The main purpose of the fluid is to protect the toad from predators. It is highly poisonous and can kill small animals like dogs or cats if they get the fluid in their mouths.

The liquid form of LSD is often soaked into blotter paper, which is then cut into tiny pieces, such as those shown here. These squares of paper are often adorned with pictures, designs, or even cartoon characters to make them more attractive to young people. But such images are misleading—LSD is a powerful and unpredictable drug. Using it just once can change the way your brain functions.

micrograms are needed to produce a high. Just one teaspoon of LSD can make 200,000 people high.

PCP is also colorless, tasteless, inexpensive to make, and easy to distribute, so it poses even more of a risk to kids than drugs like heroin or cocaine. It is sold as a capsule, powder, or liquid on the streets, and it can be smoked, swallowed, snorted (inhaled through the nose), or injected. The powder mixes well with water or alcohol, and it is sometimes mixed with dyes to make brightly colored powders and tablets. Like Naomi, many people have taken the drug without realizing it because it was mixed into their drink by someone else. Liquid PCP is also mixed with marijuana leaves and rolled into small, thin cigarettes known as loveboats. It is sometimes combined with parsley, mint, or tobacco and smoked to produce a very intense high.

Killer Drugs

As we have seen, hallucinogens like PCP and LSD are not only dangerous, but they are also unpredictable. They affect people in different ways, and they can also cause widely varying experiences in a single user. PCP can cause violent and self-destructive behavior. LSD can intensify anxiety or fear. Many deaths that occur from hallucinogen use are caused by accidents in which users drown, burn themselves, fall, step in front of moving objects, even jump out of windows to get away from their own frightening thoughts or to prove that they are invincible.

Users of hallucinogens lose judgment and awareness of their environment. Their actions while they are high are not always in their control. These effects can last up to 12 hours in LSD users and up to 6 hours in PCP users. And PCP remains active in the body 24 to 48 hours after it is taken, so users still experience effects days after taking it.

By now you are probably wondering why anyone would try drugs like LSD or PCP in the first place. In the next chapter, we'll examine the history of these drugs and how they came to be used as hallucinogens.

Humans have used hallucinogens throughout history and in all parts of the world. These peyote buttons are the dried caps of the peyote cactus, found in the U.S. Southwest. For centuries, certain Native American tribes in that region used them in religious ceremonies. Users chew the buttons or swallow them whole to experience the effects of the drug mescaline.

A HISTORY OF HALLUCINOGENS

U nlike hallucinogens such as peyote, psilocybin, and heroin, LSD and PCP are relatively new. They are also synthetic, meaning that they are not obtained from a plant or other natural source. Although the effects they have on the brain and body can be similar to naturally occurring hallucinogens, they are instead created through chemical reactions in a laboratory.

Hallucinogenic Plants

For thousands of years, Native Americans in the Southwest and desert regions of the United States have been using peyote in religious ceremonies. The histories of Greece, South America, Europe, and Asia also contain records of hallucinogen use.

It may have been animals that first demonstrated to human beings that certain kinds of plants cause altered behavior. One story describes a group of Siberian hunters who noticed reindeer behaving very oddly after eating a certain kind of mushroom. After the hunters decided to try the plant themselves, they experienced hallucinations. The sensation was so new and unusual that the hunters began harvesting and drying this type of mushroom so that they could consume it later.

Where Did LSD Come From?

Although LSD is a synthetic drug, it was designed to be similar to a substance called **ergot,** a fungus that grows on the rye plant, especially in damp conditions. Throughout history, ergot, which contains lysergic acid, was considered a very dangerous substance. During the 17th century it was the cause of many mass poisonings when rye bread containing ergot was eaten. Those who consumed a large dose of ergot often experienced intense, fiery pain, which was caused by the constriction of blood vessels in the body. In some cases, the patients' blood circulation was so strongly affected that they developed gangrene and lost their limbs.

Eventually, people made the connection between the poisonings and the amount of rye they had consumed. Still, they didn't know that small doses of ergot could cause unusual behavior. Some scientists today believe that ergot was responsible for the paranoia and hysteria that consumed small Puritan settlements in 17th-century America. Those who behaved in unusual ways were believed to be witches who were possessed by the devil, and many of them were put to death. In fact, these "witches" may have been unknowingly experiencing the toxic effects of ergot.

But ergot also seemed to have **therapeutic** value. Midwives found that ergot helped to speed up the process of giving birth and prevented new mothers from losing too much blood after they delivered their babies. Around the end of the 19th century, a number of scientific experiments were conducted to find out why ergot-infected rye had this effect, and its use as a pharmacological agent (a substance used as a medicine) increased.

In 1938, a Swiss chemist named Albert Hofmann was attempting to create a new drug to treat headaches. Knowing about ergot and its ability to help control bleeding during the birthing process, Dr. Hofmann believed that it could also be used to decrease blood flow to the brain and thus cure chronic headaches.

Hofmann succeeded in making a basic chemical very similar to the one found in ergot. He called it lysergic acid diethylamide, or LSD. Dr. Hofmann tested one version for its **analgesic** (painkilling) qualities in laboratory animals. But he noticed that although the drug didn't seem to help manage pain, it did cause strange and jittery behavior in the animals to whom he administered it. He didn't know how to interpret these effects, so he put the bottle of LSD on a shelf, where it remained for five years.

In 1943, Hofmann decided to conduct further testing with LSD. One day, he got some of it on his hands and accidentally ingested a tiny amount of it. Not long after, he began feeling what he described as "peculiarly restless" and somewhat dizzy. He felt so bad that he decided to stop working and go home for the day.

Dr. Hofmann recorded in a journal what he experienced when he got home. "I lay down and sank in a kind of drunkenness," he wrote, "which was characterized by extreme activity of imagination." He had to close his eyes because normal daylight seemed painfully bright. "An uninterrupted stream of fantasies," all of them extremely vivid and intense, with shifting colors, passed through his mind. After about two hours, he began to feel normal once more.

Three days later Dr. Hofmann decided to test whether the effects he had experienced were really from the LSD. He took what he believed was a very small amount—250 micrograms—which scientists have since discovered is about five times the dose required to produce intense hallucinations in the average person. About 40 minutes later, he noted in his journal, he felt anxious and dizzy, experienced visual disturbances and inappropriate laughing, and had difficulty concentrating.

After taking the drug, Dr. Hofmann felt unsteady enough to ask his lab technician to help him get home on his bicycle. On the way, he saw extremely bright colors and beautiful images. Dr. Hofmann's condition improved after about six hours, but he still had visual problems and everything seemed drenched in "poisonous," disagreeable colors.

By the next day, Dr. Hofmann felt normal again, but he was very shaken by what the tiny dose of this drug

A tiny drop of LSD can bring on incredible mind-altering effects. Dr. Albert Hofmann, who formulated the drug, found this out when he experimented with it. Initially, he wanted to create a headache cure that was inexpensive and easy to make. What he created was a drug that produced vivid hallucinations and left him shaken and disturbed.

had done to him. Albert Hofmann had experienced the first deliberate LSD trip. Eventually he would write about his experimentation with the drug in a book called *LSD: My Problem Child.* "I was overcome by a fear that I was going out of my mind," he wrote. "The worst part of it being that I was clearly aware of my condition. My power of observation was unimpaired. Occasionally, I felt as if I were out of my body. I thought I had died."

Hofmann wasn't sure whether LSD had therapeutic value, and instead he termed it a mood-changer. He knew that the intense side effects would prevent it from becoming a popular drug for headaches.

Over the next few years, LSD generated a great deal of interest. In 1949 American scientists began testing this exotic drug, and they fed it to spiders, fish, rats, cats, dogs, goats—even an elephant. In all of these animals, it produced extreme behavioral changes, just as Dr. Hoffman had described.

Researchers believed that because LSD had such strong effects on the mind, it might be a useful tool in treating some **psychiatric** (mental) disorders such as **schizophrenia.** They believed that since LSD made people feel as though they were "outside" of themselves, it might also help those with mental disorders see themselves more objectively. But the drug proved ineffective not only in tests with schizophrenic patients but also for alcoholics, drug addicts, and criminals. Even worse, researchers were beginning to realize that LSD also seemed to transform normal individuals into people with mild to severe mental disorders.

By the early 1960s, however, LSD became available on the street. Dr. Timothy Leary, a clinical psychologist and teacher at Harvard University, began to write about the dramatic effects he experienced when he tried the LSD-like drug psilocybin while traveling in Mexico. After experimenting further with LSD, Leary became convinced that the drug could "expand consciousness" and make people smarter and more creative. The well-respected scientist drew a great deal of attention by promoting the drug during his lectures. Along with another scientist, Dr. Richard Alpert, he encouraged regular use of LSD to develop a more creative brain.

"Turn on, tune in, drop out" became their catchphrase.

The administrators at Harvard University were not convinced by this argument, however, and both Leary and Alpert were fired in 1963. But their "campaign" to promote LSD use spread from student to student and

"Turn on, tune in, drop out" was the motto of Dr. Timothy Leary, one of the first LSD experimenters. During the 1960s, he gained a large following as a promoter of the drug. After he got into trouble over his campaign and as the popularity of LSD declined, Leary turned to designing computer-generated "hallucinations." Here he is shown in his home with video images projected around him.

from school to school. By the mid-1960s, people from all walks of life were experimenting with LSD.

By the 1970s, because scientists decided that LSD had no real use as a therapeutic drug, the Food and Drug Administration (FDA) classified LSD as a **Schedule I drug**. This means that it has a high potential for abuse and has no known medical value. Only researchers are legally permitted to use a Schedule I drug. (Other Schedule I drugs include heroin and marijuana.)

The United States quickly passed tough laws to make LSD illegal. Anyone caught manufacturing, selling, using, or possessing LSD could be fined $5,000 and spend a year in jail for a first offense.

During the 1970s, LSD use began to decline for a number of reasons. Increasing numbers of people were experiencing bad trips and reporting these trips to other users. Many users ended up in hospital emergency rooms for injuries that occurred while they were tripping or because the **flashbacks** they had were so terrifying that they wanted to make them stop. (Flashbacks are sensations of being high that occur even when a person has not recently taken the drug.) People also noticed that friends who were chronic users showed signs of depression and mental illness. LSD use also decreased because researchers began reporting that it could damage the chromosomes of people who used it, meaning that they could have children with birth defects.

Recently, though, LSD has become popular again, especially among high school and college students.

Those who study drug use believe that this has happened because a whole new generation is growing up without knowledge of what the drug does to the body and mind. They point out that today's young people weren't around in the 1960s and 1970s, when the harmful and dangerous effects of LSD were being discovered. Instead, some kids today think that LSD is an exciting, fun drug.

Another reason LSD has become popular again is that, unlike other illegal drugs such as heroin and cocaine, it is very cheap and easy to make. The strength of LSD and its rising popularity have also created nightmares for hospital emergency employees because there is no known treatment for a person who is tripping on LSD. And because the drug is often created in illegal underground chemistry labs from flammable compounds, the danger of fire is constant.

PCP: The "Dangerous Angel"

PCP was initially designed by a pharmaceutical company named Parke, Davis & Company as an **intravenous** drug (one that is injected into the veins using a hypodermic needle). It was given the **brand name** Sernyl, and early tests on animals indicated that the drug might be very useful in surgery, both as an anesthetic and as an analgesic. In 1964, when the federal government allowed the manufacturer to test the drug on humans, PCP promised to be the ideal surgical drug. Unlike other anesthetics, it did not affect breathing, it relieved pain, and it mildly stimulated the heart.

Instead of "killing" pain, it blocked the perception of pain. (This characteristic is also what makes it such a dangerous street drug, since users don't feel pain even when they have been badly injured.)

Before long, however, increasing numbers of hospital surgery patients began reporting symptoms of confusion, terror, and unpleasant hallucinations due to PCP. These hallucinations were often extremely disorienting, but they were not like those produced by LSD. Patients reported that they felt as though they were no longer within their bodies, and they sometimes felt weightless. For these reasons, PCP became less popular as a surgical drug.

Just as LSD had been tested on patients with psychological disorders, PCP was used experimentally on prisoners who had been jailed for violent crimes. But the tests were terminated when the prisoners being treated with PCP became even more agitated and violent. Finally the manufacturer of Sernyl took the drug off the market.

Somehow word spread on the street about PCP and its unusual effects. When it first appeared in San Francisco, California, it was known as the "peace pill." When they took it as a pill, however, users had trouble controlling the doses necessary to obtain only pleasant effects. Many users suffered frightening symptoms instead. Nevertheless, PCP's low cost made it an appealing alternative to other "mind-expanding" drugs such as mescaline and psychedelic mushrooms. The drug quickly earned a bad reputation among recreational users, however, and by the late 1960s, PCP tablets had all but disappeared from the streets.

The legal manufacture of PCP was discontinued in 1979, but the drug had already illegally resurfaced on the street in the 1970s, when it became available in liquid and powder form. Word had spread that PCP was relatively easy to manufacture, and in its new form it could be added to herbs, tea, tobacco, or marijuana, and smoked. This made the dosage easier to control, and users experienced the effects of the drug much more quickly. Like LSD, the drug was easy to make and distribute illegally because only a small amount was needed to get high.

Today, PCP still has a bad reputation among many drug users because its effects are unpredictable and often disturbing. Many people who try it use it only once. Others fear that it will cause mental illness if they use it regularly. The fact that PCP is easily mixed with other drugs and can go undetected makes it an extremely dangerous drug. Users of PCP often injure or kill themselves or others, especially by drowning or in bizarre accidents, while high on the drug.

In the next chapter, we'll examine the ways that hallucinogens like LSD and PCP act on the brain and body to produce these unusual effects, and how they can cause permanent damage in chronic users.

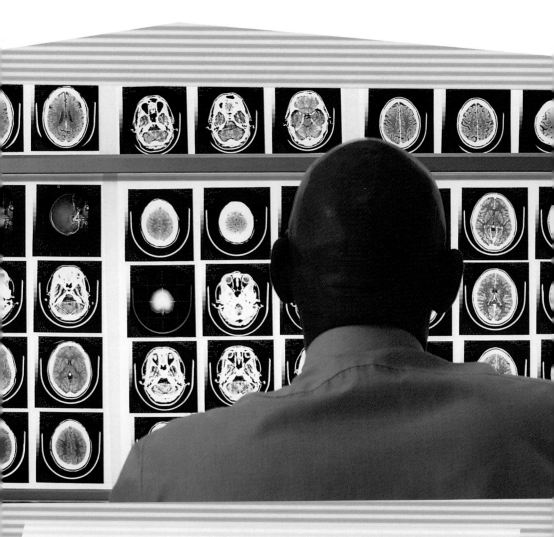

Through research and testing, scientists are learning more about how hallucinogens work and what they do to the mind and body. Researchers know that the drugs change the brain's chemistry, but it is not clear exactly how they do so. Some experts think the drugs may interfere with parts of the brain that have to do with sleeping and dreaming.

4

WHAT HALLUCINOGENS DO TO YOU

Hallucinogens work by altering the chemistry of the brain. After they are ingested, they travel through the blood to the brain, where they stimulate certain areas called **receptor sites**. These sites are located on **neurons,** the nerve cells in the brain that are responsible for transmitting messages between the brain and the body.

Neurons release chemicals called **neurotransmitters,** which carry messages between neurons to start or stop impulses in the brain. Although scientists are not exactly sure how hallucinogens work in the brain, they believe that the drugs may interfere with a number of different receptors or with neurotransmitters.

What LSD Does to Your Brain

LSD causes many things to happen in your brain. But how this drug actually works is not well understood because it is very difficult to conduct research that would allow scientists to view the areas of the brain that are affected.

LSD is thought to affect the **raphe nucleus,** which is part of the brain stem. The brain stem connects the spinal cord to the rest of the brain and controls actions that the body does automatically, such as breathing, coughing, and sneezing. Even after much research, scientists have not been able to explain how LSD alters the raphe nucleus. Some believe that LSD may decrease the activity of receptors for a neurotransmitter called **serotonin,** which is important in controlling mood and regulating eating behavior, appetite, and sleep patterns.

LSD does have a chemical structure that is similar to serotonin, but the theory that it affects serotonin receptor sites remains controversial, mainly because the actions of serotonin itself are not completely understood. Continuing research on how LSD affects neurotransmitters will help scientists better understand the way both the human brain and serotonin work.

What LSD Does to Your Mind

While the physical effects of LSD are not well defined, the psychological effects are very distinct. Users feel the effects of the drug about 30 minutes after ingesting it. Within an hour they are "flying," a sensation that may last from two to six hours. Generally, the greater the dose, the more intense the sensation. Users lose their sense of where their bodies are. They cannot tell where their arms and legs are, for example, and they don't

Some scientists believe that LSD affects the raphe nucleus, which is part of the brain stem. The brain stem, which connects the spinal cord to the rest of the brain, controls breathing, coughing, sneezing, and other actions that the body does involuntarily.

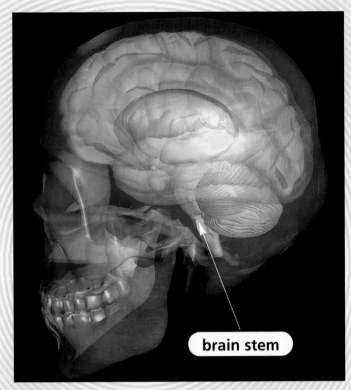

brain stem

know what is part of their body and what is not. One user said that what he thought was a chair he was sitting in was actually his own legs.

People who are high on LSD lose the ability to judge distance, size, and shape. Objects in the environment become distorted and appear to move around. Users may also experience what is called **synesthesia**, a condition in which one "sees" sounds, "hears" sights, or "tastes" odors. This sensation is what is remembered most clearly when the trip has ended and is what has caused many to think the experience has made them more creative.

Some LSD users experience unpleasant **tactile** hallucinations; for example, they may feel things crawling on their skin. Like PCP, the drug also makes the user less afraid of dangerous situations, although this effect is not as pronounced as it is with PCP.

LSD users can quickly develop a **tolerance** to the drug, meaning that they need to take increasingly larger doses to get the same effects they once got from smaller amounts. However, LSD tolerance wears off quickly; users who stop taking it will have no tolerance to it after just a few days. If users take the drug again, they may have an extremely intense trip or even overdose.

Like PCP and many other drugs, the level of intoxication of an LSD high can vary, depending on the user's mood and expectations of what the drug will do. Users who are in a bad mood to begin with may become overly aggressive or hostile while high. LSD is also known to intensify personality. Shy people become more shy, for example, or exceptionally dramatic people become even more dramatic.

LSD can also cause flashbacks. Although flashbacks usually occur among chronic users, they may also happen to people who have tried the drug only once or twice. Flashbacks can occur at any time, even when the former user feels good, and even years after taking the drug.

Scientists observe that flashbacks seem to occur more often in the moments before falling asleep. They also occur more frequently when former users are driving, drinking alcohol, or taking other drugs, or when they are in the presence of bright lights or in a crowd of people.

There are three types of flashbacks: emotional, somatic, and perceptual. Emotional flashbacks are painful and dangerous. They are much like a bad trip. Art Linkletter, a popular television entertainer in the 1960s, had a daughter who used LSD only once. She told her father she had a very bad trip and never wanted to use the drug again. Six months later, she had an emotional flashback and jumped out of the window of her high-rise building.

A somatic flashback alters the feeling of the body. Symptoms include tremors, weakness, nausea and vomiting, dizziness, and a tingling sensation on the skin. Those experiencing this type of flashback become very anxious and may not recognize the experience as a flashback; instead, they may believe that they are dying.

The least dangerous, and among LSD users the most highly desired, is the perceptual flashback. During this type of event, people experience hallucinations as though they were having a "good trip." In fact some users call this a "free trip," meaning that they did not have to take the drug again to experience it. Free trips may seem pleasant to the person who is having them, but they can be extremely dangerous if he or she is performing a task such as driving. In other situations— a job interview, for example—such experiences can be quite embarrassing.

A perceptual flashback or "free trip" can be dangerous in certain situations, such as when driving a car. Free trips can be triggered by alcohol use and exposure to bright lights.

LSD and Mental Illness

Because LSD is a psychomimetic drug, chronic use can produce a condition similar to a mental illness like schizophrenia. Users feel paranoia, as though everyone is out to get them. Repeated LSD use intensifies this experience and also causes users to be less motivated and less interested in things that previously gave them pleasure. Although LSD is not believed to cause physical dependence, chronic users can become depressed or even suicidal.

What PCP Does to Your Brain

PCP is a dissociative anesthetic, meaning that users do not perceive pain because they feel separated, or dissociated, from their bodies. A person who is high on PCP can, for example, see his hand, but not realize that it belongs to him.

As with LSD, researchers are not clear about how dissociative anesthetics work in the body. They are thought to interfere with the receptors for a neurotransmitter called **glutamate**. PCP may also block the functions of the **neocortex,** the part of the brain that controls intellect and instinct.

In addition, PCP acts as a stimulant, much like an amphetamine, by affecting receptor sites for **dopamine,** a neurotransmitter responsible for producing feelings of pleasure. The actions of PCP on the brain are extremely complicated. Scientists believe that discovering exactly how the drug works can help them learn how the brain itself functions.

What PCP Does to Your Mind

People high on PCP have been known to inflict horrible injury on themselves without feeling pain. One man who was high on PCP poked at his own eyes until he could no longer see. He remembers doing so, but he experienced no pain and so he did not stop. Police reports have recorded cases of PCP users freezing to death while exposed to bitter cold conditions without wearing clothing.

PCP abusers also pose great danger to those around them. Many cities train law enforcement officers to recognize the odd behavior that marks a PCP abuser and to approach that person very carefully. Some people who are high on PCP may feel that they have superhuman powers, and some researchers believe that this may actually make them unusually strong and therefore dangerous.

What PCP Does to Your Body

At first, PCP makes the user feel very relaxed and produces a floating sensation. In small doses, the drug increases breathing, pulse rate, and blood pressure. Users sweat and their skin becomes flushed. At higher doses, it slows down these functions. Users may experience nausea, dizziness, and vomiting. Chronic use of the drug can cause delusions, depression, weight loss, garbled speech, violent outbursts, and disorientation.

What Else Do LSD and PCP Do?

One of the most frightening and long-lasting effects of drugs like LSD and PCP is their ability to change the way your body and brain function. Users may suffer bouts of depression or anxiety for the remainder of their lives, even if they stop using the drug or use it only once. Long-term PCP users are also more likely to commit suicide and may suffer from delusions, panic attacks, and psychotic episodes. PCP users may suddenly experience episodes of confusion that last for hours—even years after they last took the drug.

In some cases users have become inactive and expressionless and remain motionless for hours. Many experts believe that this condition in PCP and LSD users is a result of brain damage. Adolescents who become chronic PCP users display a decrease in growth and development, as well as learning difficulties. Chronic adult PCP users live with lost memory, faulty perception, and poor concentration. They may hear voices that do not exist and experience PCP psychosis, including disturbed thought patterns that can last for days and weeks.

Both PCP and LSD are believed to destroy memories of past events and the ability to learn new things. As a result, chronic users of these drugs may end up being completely changed from their former selves.

Why Do People Use Hallucinogens and Other Illegal Drugs?

After learning about what hallucinogens can do to people, you may wonder why anyone would even try these substances. If you were to ask users of PCP or LSD why they take these drugs, they might tell you that they want to have a new experience or try new ways of thinking and feeling. They may claim that they feel more connected to the earth and to God, or that the drug has enlightened them and changed their viewpoints. This may explain the actions of people such as Dr. Timothy Leary, who used LSD so often that his

It's tough to stand out from the crowd. The desire to fit in is one of the strongest influences on teenagers. Rejection by others can make teens feel lonely, confused, or depressed. These feelings may lead some kids to take drugs. But as you now know, taking drugs can create a whole new set of problems.

thought processes eventually became garbled and illogical. But chronic users nearly always use these drugs to escape from the pressures and problems of everyday life, which is one of the reasons people use illegal drugs of any kind.

Another reason kids turn to drugs is that they feel that they need to do so to fit in with their friends or classmates. This is an example of peer pressure. The desire to fit in can be a very powerful feeling, but you don't *have* to give in to peer pressure. There are ways to avoid doing things you don't want to do while still feeling like part of the gang. Besides, chances are you're not the only one in the group who doesn't want to take drugs. Others may feel the same way, but they may also be afraid to speak up. But if you want to do what's best for you, you have to stand up for yourself.

This isn't always easy, of course. It takes courage. You may fear that you'll lose your friends. But you may find that if you do say no, other friends who may have been fearful of not fitting in will take your side because they'll know they are not alone. And it's often easier than you might think to say "No, thanks."

Imagine that you took LSD only once when you were in seventh grade. Years later, while you are driving a car by yourself for the first time or standing at the front of a church during your wedding, you suddenly have a terrifying flashback. Perhaps flashbacks make LSD the scariest drug of all. Maybe it is the feeling of being indestructible that makes PCP so frightening. Or maybe it is the fact that one dose of either of these drugs can change the way your brain works for the rest of your life. In any case, using LSD or PCP just once will change your life, and not for the better. Before you decide to try drugs as a way to escape your problems, find a new way to think or fit in with your friends. Think very hard about what you will end up doing to your brain and body. It only takes one dose to change everything.

In the next chapter, we will discuss some of the ways that you can stay healthy and say no to drug use. We will also look at ways you can get help for yourself or for a friend or relative who uses drugs.

You don't have to ruin your life by using drugs. There are many ways teens can get help with drug problems. Seeking support and advice from a trusted adult—a counselor, teacher, or close relative—is a first step.

HOW TO GET HELP

N ow that you know about the harmful effects of hallucinogens like LSD and PCP, you need to know how to protect yourself and your friends from these drugs. In this chapter, we will learn how you can say no to peer pressure and stay drug-free. We'll look at some of the ways you can recognize the signs that someone you know may be abusing hallucinogens or other drugs. Finally, we'll find out where you can get help for your friends, your relatives, or yourself.

People who have used hallucinogens sometimes have trouble becoming drug-free not because the drugs are addictive but because of the situations in which they have used the drugs. Hallucinogen users commonly take such drugs in social settings along with other users, who may also be friends. In case the users have a bad trip, a friend is there to help or to prevent them from harming themselves. For these reasons, giving up these drugs can be very difficult, especially when others around the former user are still getting high while he or she is trying to quit.

Hallucinogen users who want to quit often need psychological help to change the way they view their lives and to help them remove themselves from destructive situations. Many times people who abuse drugs don't feel good about themselves or have lost their outside interests, friends, or even a job. These situations can contribute to low self-worth. In this position, the user is very likely to go back to taking the drug because it seems to be the easiest way to solve problems.

Getting Help

Psychiatrists have a medical degree (M.D.) with a specialty in treating mental illness. They can prescribe drugs and medication. Psychologists have a degree in psychology (the study of human behavior) but cannot prescribe drugs. Both kinds of specialists, however, can be extremely helpful in changing the behavior of LSD or PCP users. Through counseling in a rehabilitation program, these professionals can help users change behavior patterns and negative thoughts. This treatment can help users stop taking drugs and help them to establish a healthy way of life.

Admitting that you need help with a drug problem can be scary. And realizing that you cannot solve your problem alone may feel overwhelming. But anyone who is abusing drugs requires experienced help. A good counselor, coach, teacher, or other adult you feel comfortable talking to can direct you to the right support group or treatment program.

The best drug treatment program for each person depends on many factors, including the individual's personality, social situation, age, family situation, and degree and length of drug use. No treatment can guarantee a cure, but all of them offer hope to people who feel as though drugs have taken over their lives.

Most drug treatment programs fit into one of the following categories:

Self-help programs—free, drop-in meetings tailored to specific addictions. Participants listen to others speak about their drug or alcohol abuse. Examples include Alcoholics Anonymous and Narcotics Anonymous.

Outpatient treatment—a structured plan of individual and group counseling that often includes family counseling. This kind of treatment is especially useful for young drug abusers at an early stage of addiction, or for those who are at low risk of relapsing (returning to drug abuse).

Day treatment—a daylong program of intense counseling, after which the patient returns home. This type of treatment is best for former drug abusers who are not at great risk for relapsing and are able to live at home rather than in a treatment facility.

Inpatient treatment—a highly structured program in which patients stay in a hospital-like facility and participate in intensive counseling and treatment over a period of weeks or months.

Residential treatment—a supervised, round-the-clock treatment program in which patients live at a center for up to a year. This kind of program is best for people who are at great risk of relapsing.

How Can You Avoid LSD, PCP, and Other Drugs?

Now you understand the dangers of LSD and PCP. You know that using them just once can change your life. Wouldn't it be awful if you cut your hair and even though you hated the new style, it never grew back? Or if you ate too much candy once and never felt better again? That is just how these drugs can work. They can change your brain, and they can alter your life. You will not only hurt those who love you, but you will also hurt yourself.

Problems with alcohol and other drugs usually begin in adolescence. In fact, these are the most common health problems that teens face. Many teenage deaths are the result of accidents and suicide caused by using drugs. Using drugs can make any family or school problem worse.

Some people your age don't worry about this. They may try to talk you into using drugs by convincing you that trying a substance once won't hurt you. Don't give

Often people who abuse drugs are having difficult times or have low self-esteem. Although the best drug treatment program for each person depends on various factors, many hallucinogen users who want to quit need profes-sional psychological help to change the way they view their lives.

in to peer pressure. You will experience it all your life, and now is a very good time to take a stand. The sooner you learn how to protect yourself from harmful drugs, the easier it will be to turn them down later in life.

You may be thinking that this is very easy to say, but not easy to do. The best way to avoid peer pressure

How to Tell If You Have a Drug Problem

Drug and alcohol problems affect all kinds of people, regardless of age, sex, race, income level, or way of life. If you abuse drugs or alcohol and think you're not like others who do, you're wrong. Just like anyone else who abuses drugs, you can seriously endanger your body and mind—and even your life. To find out whether you have a problem, try to answer the following questions honestly:

- Can I predict the next time I will use drugs or get drunk?
- Do I think that I need alcohol or other drugs to have fun?
- Do I turn to alcohol or other drugs to make myself feel better after an argument or confrontation?
- Do I have to drink more or use more drugs to get the same effect I once felt with a smaller amount?
- Do I drink alcohol or use other drugs when I'm alone?
- When I drink alcohol or use other drugs, do I forget certain segments of time?
- Am I having trouble at work or school because of alcohol or other drug use?
- Do I make promises to others or to myself to stop drinking alcohol or using other drugs, but then break them?
- Do I feel alone, scared, miserable, or depressed?

If you answered yes to any of the above questions, you may have a drug problem. Don't be discouraged, though. You are not alone. Millions of people around the world have triumphed over drug abuse and are now living healthy, drug-free lives.

to use drugs is to find friends with similar interests who also want to stay drug-free. If you stay away from people who use drugs, you can often avoid feeling pressured to take drugs. Remember, if your friends are using drugs, they may be doing so because they also feel insecure. They may seem cool to you, but they just want to fit in too. And if they convince you to join them, they won't feel so bad about themselves.

Here are some easy ways to avoid using drugs:

- Skip going to places where you know there will be alcohol and other drugs.

- Seek out friends who are not drug users.

- Find things to do after school and on weekends that make you feel good about yourself and increase your skills. Take art or music classes. You don't have to be good at these things. If you like them, you will get better at them and have fun doing it. The skills you develop now may also come in handy later in life.

- Organize a drug awareness program in your school, church, or community.

Most of all, do everything you can to feel good about yourself. And remember: although it seems like "everyone" is using drugs, they are not. A national survey taken in 1997 showed that less than 4 percent of kids aged 12 and 13 had ever used illegal drugs. That means that more than 96 percent of them *never* used illegal drugs.

The help and support of good friends can make a big difference if you feel pressured to use drugs. Seek friends who feel the same way you do about not using drugs. It's easier to turn down harmful substances when you're with others who want to stay drug-free.

How Can I Tell If Someone I Know Is Using Drugs?

If you know people who are using drugs, you can help. If some of your friends are avoiding you or giving up their normal activities like sports or church, they may be having trouble with alcohol or other drugs.

They may lie to you and tell you they don't do drugs because they don't want you to know. Or they may be constantly talking about all of the alcohol or other drugs they used last weekend. They may actually be asking for your help this way.

It is not always easy to tell if a friend or relative is using LSD or PCP, but there are a few signs you can look for if you suspect that they are. Look for odd behavior, mood swings, weight loss, absentminded-ness, sleepiness, and paranoid thinking. If you think that a friend or family member is using drugs, talk to an adult whom you trust—a teacher, baby-sitter, coach, minister, relative, or parent. You may feel disloyal doing this, but the truth is that you are being a good friend.

Remember that when your friend does seek help, you should be as kind and as supportive as possible. He or she will be going through one of life's most difficult experiences and will need your understanding and encouragement.

As a young adult, you can make a big difference in your life and in the lives of those around you by avoiding drugs. The world is a huge place with lots of great things to experience and learn. You won't need drugs to succeed. Just go have fun and believe in yourself.

GLOSSARY

acetylcholine—a brain chemical that regulates many of the body's activities that keep us alive, such as breathing and digestion.

amphetamine—a type of drug that stimulates the central nervous system, increasing energy levels and sleeplessness, sometimes causing dangerous side effects.

analgesic—a substance that causes insensitivity to pain.

anesthetic—a substance that causes loss of feeling or consciousness and therefore helps in relieving pain.

atropine—a belladonna alkaloid found in plants like jimsonweed. Very small doses of this hallucinogenic compound are sometimes used to treat asthma or stomach problems, but in high doses it can be deadly.

autonomic—acting or occurring involuntarily. The autonomic nervous system controls body functions such as breathing, sweating, and digestion.

bad trip—an unpleasant experience that results from taking LSD, usually involving frightening sounds, feelings, or hallucinations.

belladonna alkaloid—a hallucinogenic compound found in the belladonna family of plants that can shut down important body activities and cause the heart and lungs to function improperly.

brand name—a specific name under which a product is marketed and sold. For example, Bayer is one of many brand names for aspirin.

bufotenine—a hallucinogen secreted by the cane and Colorado River toads that raises blood pressure and heart rate and can cause paralysis.

bummer—a bad LSD or PCP high. Bummers produce frightening images and cause paranoia in the user. Most flashbacks are bummers.

dissociative anesthetic—a substance that causes the user to become completely out of touch with, or dissociated from, his or her environment. PCP is a dissociative anesthetic.

dissociative state—a condition in which a person is completely out of touch with his or her environment. Some hallucinogens produce a dissociative state in the user.

DMT—dimethyltryptamine; a synthetic hallucinogen that produces a brief high similar to that of LSD.

dopamine—a neurotransmitter in the brain. Dopamine is released by neurons in the limbic system, a part of the brain that controls feelings of pleasure.

ergot—a fungus that grows on the rye plant and contains the hallucinogen lysergic acid.

flashback—also known as a "free trip," the occurrence of an LSD high even though the user has not taken the drug recently. Flashbacks can occur at any time, even years after using LSD. Recurring flashbacks occur mainly in people who have taken LSD many times.

glutamate—a neurotransmitter believed to be affected by PCP.

hallucination—an object or vision that is not real but is perceived by a person as real.

hallucinogen—a substance, such as LSD and PCP, that distorts the user's perceptions or causes the user to perceive objects or visions that are not real.

intravenous—introduced into the body through a vein.

ketamine—a drug, originally used as an anesthetic, that causes the user to be unaware of the environment and unresponsive to pain.

LSD—lysergic acid diethylamide, a synthetic hallucinogenic drug similar to a fungus called ergot that grows on the rye plant.

MDA—methylenedioxyamphetamine; a hallucinogenic drug.

mescaline—a hallucinogenic drug derived from the peyote cactus plant.

neocortex—the area of the brain that controls intellect and instinct.

neuron—a nerve cell.

neurotransmitter—a chemical that is released by neurons and carries messages between them.

paranoia—extreme, irrational distrust of others, accompanied by exaggerated fears.

PCP—phencyclidine; sometimes called "angel dust"; an animal tranquilizer that is sometimes mixed with marijuana or other drugs. PCP is extremely dangerous; even one use can cause serious mental illness.

peyote—a type of cactus plant from which the hallucinogen mescaline is derived.

potent—powerful.

psilocin—a compound in *Psilocybe mexicana* and *Psilocybe cyanescens* mushrooms that is responsible for their hallucinogenic properties.

psilocybin—a hallucinogenic compound in *Psilocybe mexicana* and *Psilocybe cyanescens* mushrooms.

psychedelic—a term coined in the 1950s to describe hallucinogenic substances.

psychiatric—concerning mental, emotional, or behavioral disorders.

psychosis—mental illness that is usually characterized by loss of contact with reality.

psychotomimetic drug—a substance that produces a state similar to mental illness.

raphe nucleus—a part of the brain stem, which connects the spinal cord to the rest of the brain. The raphe nucleus controls automatic functions such as breathing, coughing, and sneezing. LSD is believed to affect the raphe nucleus.

receptor site—a special area of a cell that combines with a chemical substance to alter the cell's function.

Schedule I drug—a drug that is considered unsafe to use, has no known medical value, and has a high potential for abuse. Marijuana, LSD, and heroin are Schedule I drugs.

schizophrenia—a mental disorder marked by loss of contact with the environment, a decreased ability to function in everyday life, and disintegration of personality.

scopolamine—a belladonna alkaloid found in plants like jimsonweed.

serotonin—a neurotransmitter involved in the control of mood, aggression, and sexual behavior.

STP—a synthetic hallucinogen that is chemically related to amphetamines.

synesthesia—a confusion of the five senses that occurs as a result of consuming high doses of certain hallucinogens. A person who is high on LSD, for example, may "see" sounds and "hear" colors.

synthetic—made by people rather than found in nature. Hallucinogens such as LSD and PCP are synthetic drugs.

tactile—relating to touch.

therapeutic—providing or assisting in a cure.

tolerance—a condition in which a drug user needs increasing amounts of the drug to achieve the same level of intoxication previously obtained from using smaller amounts.

toxic—poisonous.

trip—the "high" experienced by a user of hallucinogenic drugs.

BIBLIOGRAPHY

Carroll, Marilyn. *PCP: The Dangerous Angel.* Philadelphia: Chelsea House Publishers, 1992.

Center for Substance Abuse Prevention (CSAP). "Tips for Teens About Hallucinogens." NCADI Publication No. PHD642. Rockville, MD: CSAP, 1996.

Furst, Peter T. *Mushrooms: Psychedelic Fungi.* Philadelphia: Chelsea House Publishers, 1992.

Kuhn, Cynthia, Scott Swartzwelder, and Wilkie Wilson. *Buzzed: The Straight Facts About the Most Used and Abused Drugs from Alcohol to Ecstasy.* New York: W. W. Norton & Co., 1998.

Myers, Arthur. *Drugs and Peer Pressure.* New York: Rosen Publishing Group, 1995.

National Clearinghouse for Alcohol and Drug Information (NCADI), Center for Substance Abuse Prevention. *Drugs of Abuse.* NCADI Publication No. RP0926. Rockville, MD: NCADI, 1998.

———. *Just the Facts.* NCADI Publication No. RP0884. Rockville, MD: NCADI, 1996.

———. *Recovery from Substance Abuse and Addiction: Real People Tell Their Stories.* NCADI Publication No. PHD749. Rockville, MD: NCADI, 1998.

———. *You Can't Change the Past But You Can Choose the Future.* NCADI Publication No. MS609. Rockville, MD: NCADI, 1997.

National Institute on Drug Abuse (NIDA). *Mind Over Matter: The Brain's Response to Hallucinogens.* NCADI Publication No. PHD803. Rockville, MD: NIDA, 1997.

Trulson, Michael E. *LSD: Visions or Nightmares?* Philadelphia: Chelsea House Publishers, 1992.

FIND OUT MORE ABOUT HALLUCINOGENS AND DRUG ABUSE

The following list includes agencies, organizations, and websites that provide information about LSD, PCP, and other drugs of abuse. You can also find out where to go for help with a drug problem.

Many national organizations have local chapters listed in your phone directory. Look under "Drug Abuse and Addiction" to find resources in your area.

Agencies and Organizations in the United States

American Council for Drug Education
164 West 74th Street
New York, NY 10023
212-758-8060
800-488-DRUG (3784)
http://www.acde.org/
wlittlefield

Center for Substance Abuse Treatment
Information and Treatment Referral Hotline
11426-28 Rockville Pike, Suite 410
Rockville, MD 20852
800-662-HELP (4357)

Eden Children's Project
1035 Franklin Avenue East
Minneapolis, MN 55404
612-874-9441

Marin Institute for the Prevention of Alcohol and Other Drug Problems
24 Belvedere Street
San Rafael, CA 94901
415-456-5692

Narcotics Anonymous (NA)
P.O. Box 9999
Van Nuys, CA 91409
818-773-9999

National Center on Addiction and Substance Abuse at Columbia University
152 West 57th Street, 12th Floor
New York, NY 10019-3310
212-841-5200
212-956-8020
http://www.casacolumbia.org/home.htm

National Clearinghouse for Alcohol and Drug Information (NCADI)
P.O. Box 2345
Rockville, MD 20847-2345
800-729-6686
800-487-4889 TDD
800-HI-WALLY (449-2559, Children's Line)
http://www.health.org/

National Council on Alcoholism and Drug Dependence (NCADD)

12 West 21st St., 7th Floor
New York, NY 10017
212-206-6770
800-NCA-CALL (622-2255)
http://www.ncadd.org/

National Crime Prevention Council

1700 K Street, N.W., 2nd Floor
Washington, DC 20006
202-466-6272

National Families in Action

2296 Henderson Mill Road, Suite 300
Atlanta, GA 30345
404-934-6364

Office of National Drug Control Policy

750 17th Street, N.W., 8th Floor
Washington, DC 20503
http://www.whitehousedrugpolicy.gov/ondcp
888-395-NDCP (6327)

Parents' Resource Institute for Education (PRIDE)

3610 DeKalb Technology Parkway, Suite 105
Atlanta, GA 30340
770-458-9900
http://www.prideusa.org/

Agencies and Organizations in Canada

Addictions Foundation of Manitoba

1031 Portage Avenue
Winnipeg, Manitoba R3G 0R8
204-944-6277
http://www.mbnet.mb.ca/crm/health/afm.html

Addiction Research Foundation

33 Russell Street
Toronto, Ontario M5S 2S1
416-595-6100
800-463-6273 in Ontario

Alberta Alcohol and Drug Abuse Commission

10909 Jasper Avenue, 6th Floor
Edmonton, Alberta T5J 3M9
http://www.gov.ab.ca/aadac/

British Columbia Prevention Resource Centre

96 East Broadway, Suite 211
Vancouver, British Columbia V5T 1V6
604-874-8452
800-663-1880 in British Columbia

Canadian Centre on Substance Abuse

75 Albert Street, Suite 300
Ottawa, Ontario K1P 5E7
613-235-4048
http://www.ccsa.ca/

Ontario Healthy Communities Central Office

180 Dundas Street West, Suite 1900
Toronto, Ontario M5G 1Z8
416-408-4841
http://www.opc.on.ca/ohcc/

Saskatchewan Health Resource Centre

T.C. Douglas Building
3475 Albert Street
Regina, Saskatchewan S4S 6X6
306-787-3090

Websites

Avery Smartcat's Facts & Research on Children Facing Drugs
http://www.averysmartcat.com/druginfo.htm

D.A.R.E. (Drug Abuse Resistance Education) for Kids
http://www.dare-america.com/index2.htm

Elks Drug Awareness Resource Center
http://www.elks.org/drugs/

Hazelden Foundation
http://www.hazelden.org/

Join Together Online
http://www.jointogether.org/sa/

National Institute on Drug Abuse (NIDA)
http://www.nida.nih.gov

Partnership for a Drug-Free America
http://www.drugfreeamerica.org/

Reality Check
http://www.health.org/reality/

Substance Abuse and Mental Health Services Administration (SAMHSA)
http://www.samhsa.gov

U.S. Department of Education Safe and Drug-Free Schools Program
http://inet.ed.gov/offices/OESE/SDFS

U.S. Department of Justice Kids' Page
http://www.usdoj.gov/kidspage/

Despite what you may have heard,
selling illegal drugs will not make you rich.

In 1998, two professors, Steven Levitt from the University of Chicago and Sudhir Venkatesh from Harvard University, released a study of how drug gangs make and distribute money. To get accurate information, Venkatesh actually lived with a drug gang in a midwestern city.

You may be surprised to find out that the average street dealer makes just about $3 an hour. You'd make more money working at McDonald's! Still think drug-dealing is a cool way to make money? What other after-school jobs carry the risk of going to prison or dying in the street from a gunshot wound?

Drug-dealing is illegal, and it kills people. If you're thinking of selling drugs or you know someone who is, ask yourself this question: is $3 an hour worth dying for or being imprisoned?

WHAT A DRUG GANG MAKES IN A MONTH*

	During a Gang War	No Gang War
INCOME (money coming in)	$ 44,500	$ 58,900
Other income (including dues and blackmail money)	10,000	18,000
TOTAL INCOME	**$ 54,500**	**$ 76,900**
EXPENSES (money paid out)		
Cost of drugs sold	$ 11,300	$ 12,800
Wages for officers and street pushers	25,600	37,600
Weapons	3,000	1,600
Tributes (fees) paid to central gang	5,800	5,900
Funeral expenses	2,300	800
Other expenses	8,000	3,400
TOTAL EXPENSES	**$ 56,000**	**$ 62,100**
TOTAL INCOME	$ 54,500	$ 76,900
MINUS TOTAL EXPENSES	- 56,000	- 62,100
TOTAL AMOUNT OF PROFIT IN ONE MONTH	**- 1,500**	**14,800**

* adapted from "Greedy Bosses," Forbes, August 24, 1998, p. 53.
Source: Levitt and Venkatesh.

INDEX

PICTURE CREDITS

page
12: Erika Larsen
17: Erika Larsen
20: Erika Larsen
22: Erika Larsen
26: AP/Wide World Photos
31: AP/Wide World Photos
32: Sinclair Stammers/Science Photo Library/Photo Researchers, Inc.
34: George Post/Science Photo Library/Photo Researchers, Inc.
39: Corbis Images MED2033
41: AP/Wide World Photos
46: Corbis Images MED2045
49: LifeArt Image ©1998 Williams & Wilkins
52: Erika Larsen
56: Eyewire ETE_068
58: Eyewire ETE_025
63: Eyewire ETE_027
66: Eyewire ETE_094

JANE ELLEN PHILLIPS earned a Masters of Science in Nutritional Biochemistry at Drexel University and a Ph.D. in Biochemistry at MCP (Hahnemann School of Medicine). She is currently a Research Fellow in the Cardiovascular and Pulmonary Research Institute at Allegheny General Hospital. Dr. Phillips is the recipient of a research grant from the Pennsylvania affiliate of the American Heart Association, for which she works in a volunteer capacity. She lives in Pittsburgh with her three very, very old chihuahuas.

BARRY R. McCAFFREY is Director of the Office of National Drug Control Policy (ONDCP) at the White House and a member of President Bill Clinton's cabinet. Before taking this job, General McCaffrey was an officer in the U.S. Army. He led the famous "left hook" maneuver of Operation Desert Storm that helped the United States win the Persian Gulf War.

STEVEN L. JAFFE, M.D., received his psychiatry training at Harvard University and the Massachusetts Mental Health Center and his child psychiatry training at Emory University. He has been editor of the *Newsletter of the American Academy of Child and Adolescent Psychiatry* and chairman of the Continuing Education Committee of the Georgia Psychiatric Physicians' Association. Dr. Jaffe is professor of child and adolescent psychiatry at Emory University. He is also clinical professor of psychiatry at Morehouse School of Medicine, and the director of Adolescent Substance Abuse Programs at Charter Peachford Hospital in Atlanta, Georgia.